The Powow River Anthology

The Powow River Anthology

edited by Alfred Nicol

Ocean Publishing
Flagler Beach, Florida

The Powow River Anthology

Published by:
Ocean Publishing
Post Office Box 1080
Flagler Beach, FL 32136-1080
email: oceanpublisher@cfl.rr.com
www.ocean-publishing.com

Composition by Alfred Nicol
The text of this book is composed in New Baskerville
Book Design and Cover Design by Alfred Nicol
Cover Photograph: K.D. Talbot, www.ghostflowers.com
Acknowledgments for individual poems begin on page 135

ISBN-10, print edition   0-9767291-5-6
ISBN-13   978-09767291-5-0

Library of Congress Control Number   2005938143

Printed and bound in the United States of America

For Rhina Espaillat

———————

With thanks

To The Newburyport Public Library
for providing us a place to gather every month
for all these many years,

To The Newburyport Art Association
for opening its gallery space to our reading series,
to our legendary audiences there
(famous for near-Elizabethan listening skill),
to Alfred Moskowitz, who arranges everything,

And to The Yankee Printer of Hampton, NH,
especially Ed McNamara,
for such gladly-given, generous advice and help
in putting this book together.

Contents

Introduction: *"the breathing of the Muse"*

The Powow River Poets, not to be confused with Native American powwows, derive their name from a tributary of the Merrimack River that flows through extensive wetlands where birds and wild mammals abound. As you can see from the anthology in your hands, this fecund area and its neighboring town of Newburyport have produced almost more poets than you could shake a stick at, if you ever wanted to.

A sometime visitor to Newburyport, I have always found it an impressive place. An historic seaside town of 17,000, where merchants who traded with China and builders of clipper ships built imposing mansions, it lures tourists with its funky shops and atmospheric eateries, and moreover, it crackles with creative life. Several art galleries call it home, as do some new and used bookshops and at least a couple of theater companies. It even sustains its own Arts Association, whose downtown gallery hosts exhibitions and a monthly reading series run by the Powow River Poets.

Although the activities of the River Poets center in Newburyport, not all its members are Newburyporters. In fact, only four live there; another four, in nearby Amesbury, Newbury, Haverhill, and Rowley; the rest, in Massachusetts and New Hampshire places as far away as fifty miles. "It's amazing how cohesive the group is, when our homes are so scattered!" says Rhina P. Espaillat, who, without ever being elected to office, has long been (may she forgive some rudely mixed metaphors) a sparkplug of the group, a kind of bardic queen bee or aesthetic den-mother, a teacher by vocation and by nature and, as many of her fellow poets will attest, a generous friend. At any rate, the PRP didn't exist before her time, nor had the Newburyport Arts Association made much noise until she, a former New York City teacher, and her husband, sculptor Alfred Moskowitz, came to town in 1990.

Shortly thereafter the Powow River Poets started meeting at one another's homes to exchange mutual support and to swap poems. Besides Espaillat, among the early members who still participate are Elaine Kimball, Len Krisak, and Greg Perry. Some presentday members developed their skills within the group; others, like David Berman, had cultivated their art well before the group began, then, finding it congenial, joined. The Powow River Poets are intimately acquainted with the Newburyport Arts Association, whose gallery hosts their monthly reading series, and to its glory, the Association sponsors an annual poetry contest whose prestige extends far beyond town. Astonishingly, the latest round of this contest drew 634 entries from forty states, Finland, and Canada. Judges have included Richard Moore, Joseph DeRoche, Thomas Carper, David Berman, Diana Der-Hovanessian, Bruce Bennett, Robert Shaw, Charles Martin, William Jay Smith,

Lewis Turco, and me—all of whom have read to Powow audiences. (For more information on the contest, and how slightly to enrich your coffers, see the website <www.newburyportart.org/pages/about_poets.html> and click on "Poetry Contest".) From experience, I can affirm that Powow audiences are a wonderfully friendly and intelligent bunch. Though largely made up of poets, they listen appreciatively, not even whispering—as audiences of poets sometimes do— "Huh! What's this bozo got that I don't have?" And it seems that the long and healthy survival of the PRP has been due to the fact that its members have a certain affection for one another, strive to write the best poems they can, and unselfishly rejoice whenever a fellow member sells a poem to a magazine. Some of their members—Espaillat, A. M. Juster, Len Krisak, Alfred Nicol, Deborah Warren— have published award-winning books of their own.

All this history is only to suggest that the present anthology didn't just rise out of the air like some genii or apparition. It has sprung from a nourishing environment, human contacts, and plenty of good-natured argument over how a line ought to stand. Editor Nicol must have had a tough job deciding what to put in, but to his credit, the group's variety and integrity have been preserved. Still, you might find this a radical book, for among its two dozen poets I count 17 who write in meter and/or rhyme at least some of the time. This devotion to elements of poetry that prevailed up until the Beat revolution of the early 1960s, is to say the least unusual nowadays. But if Newburyport seems a capital of enlightened craftsmanship (hostile critics might call it a cesspool of reaction), still, free verse Powow poets, too, are not merely tolerated but acclaimed. Witness the many strong open-form poems in these pages: Lois Frankenberger's "Kaddish," Merrill Kaitz's "Blue Antelope Elegy," Nancy Bailey Miller's "Grief." There are admirable stanzaic (or partly stanzaic) poems such as Karen Nelson's "Flamenco Dancer," the work of Brian T. O'Brien, and José Edmundo Ocampo Reyes's "Paálam, Wallace, Paálam"— but these are poems unfettered by strict formal patterns. In Richard Wollman's lovely "The Evidence of Things Unseen," lines vary in length as a mechanical eye dropped into a river by the underwater explorer Cousteau unexpectedly bursts, failing to ruffle a pool

> *where Petrarch had a vision,*
> *real as his own breath,*
> *and in his seclusion must have known*
> *why the eye is a sad traveler.*

You might expect some venturesome experiments in writing to be fostered in the Powow region. After all, Newburyport was once home to that famous self-styled nobleman, Lord Timothy Dexter, who published his own prose book without punctuation, but with pages of commas, periods, and exclamation marks at the back "so that the reader may salt and pepper it however he will."

The Catholicism of this anthology (with a small c, there) strikes me as just. Poetry is a house of many rooms, and whether a poet rhymes or doesn't rhyme surely matters less than whether he or she writes with sufficient energy to seize readers and strum on their emotions and keep them reading to the bottom of the poem. This rough test, all the Powow River Poets pass with unfurled colors. I haven't even mentioned any of the remarkable poems, conventional only in their formality, that strike me as worth rereading many times — David Berman's "After a Family Reunion," Bill Coyle's "Anima," Robert Crawford's "A Row of Stones," Rhina P. Espaillat's "Encounter," Midge Goldberg's "The Fish," A. M. Juster's "Cancer Prayer," Len Krisak's "Birds from Afar," Mildred Nash's "North Country Graveyard," Alfred Nicol's "Potatoes," Deborah Warren's "The Crabapple in Flower" — but this is to cite a mere sampling of the riches that these and other Powow River Poets will provide.

Enough. Browse in this book, live with it, discover for yourself its generous rewards.

— *X. J. Kennedy*

David Berman

After a Family Reunion

1

I left the party early (did they think
It rude?) before I could be bored into
Untoward remarks, before I had a drink
Too many. I had rendered what was due
Homage to common ancestry, although
I liked exchanging gossip, jokes and quips.
All "solid citizens" with what to show
For their success—cars, clothes, club memberships—

My cousins whom I played with as a child
Were almost middle-aged; their children played
Or were themselves too old to play and whiled
The time away observing our charade,
In which the players did not seek to win
And only failed at what they might have been.

2

What happened? Early marriage took its toll;
The lure of money quick and green enthralled;
One staggered bright-eyed into alcohol;
Our handsome would-be minister was called
To "PR" work, and when his soul was pledged

Beyond redemption, started preaching to
The sexually underprivileged
A gospel of libido, neither new

Nor true. And when they asked me what I did
"Up there in Boston," I was vague. "I write,"
I said, and straightway stood alone amid
My relatives. At almost but not quite
Forty, I had no wife, no house, scant pride,
Nothing to show and even less to hide.

3

The eastbound traffic, lighter than the west,
Moves toward New England, toward the last pale light
To bathe the sea, toward solitude and rest,
Away from summer on this summer night.
I drive to the continuo of Bach's
Chorales and preludes, weary of desiring
Whatever is secured with foolproof locks,
Whatever ought to be beyond aspiring.

The east is dark now; hinting of a storm,
The air outside grows cooler, fresher, more
Impatient, and the trees, though still as warm,
Cry out for motion. Shall I put up for
The night at some motel or drive on toward
The nighttime sea, the darkness of the Lord?

David Berman

_____

Disjunctures

To ward off loneliness, you pay a price
Or do not pay and suffer the disease,
And either way you make a sacrifice.

If loneliness means dying by degrees,
Involvement in another's personhood
Means giving up part of your own to please

An otherness, to be misunderstood
Or understood down to the innermost,
And either circumstance is less than good.

You may be lonely even with a host
Of friends or in a sweetheart's company,
But one truly alone becomes engrossed

In too much self or errant roles that he
Plays as a twosome, dancing with a ghost
Whose flesh he fondles inappeasably.

You deem that life disgusting? Pay the price
Or be disgusted. You will not live twice:
Be free in hell or chained in paradise.

David Berman

Future Imperfect

It will be autumn, autumn in New England;
It will be morning, morning almost noon;
The road will curve from green to gold-vermillion;
The road will curve but one curve come too soon

And out of nowhere as if you had taken
The curve too fast and overshot the rim,
You will remember someone who loved autumn,
Remember that you shared it once with him.

David Berman

Progressions of the Mind

1

"Our coloured lady," as my mother called
Her part-time maid, would talk to me about
The Bible and her church. When summer stalled
Until it seemed sheer folly to go out
And face the Southern heat, I followed her
Around the house, absorbed at least a bit
Of what she had to say, though some things were
Beyond my understanding. One thing hit
Me plain, however: she believed that those
Who went to Hell retained full memory
Of earthly life that would not decompose
And knew they were not where they wished to be,
While those in Heaven could not recognize
Themselves or others seen with Heavenly eyes.

2

Themselves or others seen with Heavenly eyes
They knew as angels—is there not a verse
In *Matthew* that implies that marriage dies
When spouses do? She asked what could be worse
For bliss than watching through eternity
Your child or mama suffering in Hell,

However justly earned that place might be,
And then she answered as if to dispel
All doubt, "The saints ain't gonna suffer there;
The Lord won't let that happen." Too young to
Dispute her logic, still I felt somewhere
Within, that what she said did not ring true
But lacked the words to ask, "How can one be
Immortal who forgets mortality?"

3

How can one be immortal who forgets
Mortality? I never quite forgot
What she had said; long after she had left—
Few maids outstayed a year and, like as not,
Deserted for the snowbirds in December—
I found out that her father and one son
Had both served time. For what I don't remember.
She must have thought whatever they had done
Would keep them out of Heaven. Back then, black
Churches leaned upon such women for
Existence; it made sense to say, "Alack,
The men who love and hurt you, who ignore
Your summons to repent—once you have died,
You will forget them on the other side."

4

You will forget them on the other side—
One who makes sociology out of
Religion will find both unjustified:
Not only the oppressed know that they love
Some who, if there is Heaven, likely will
Be going elsewhere, all denial spent,
Nor are the persons Hellbound always male.
To love on earth is never to relent;
Love bears it out beyond the edge of doom.
Is Heaven different? Could a mother bear
To hear her child gasp in another room
Forever barred to her and just not care?
If to be saved is to go on like this,
Hell's blight is no more harsh than Heaven's bliss.

5

Hell's blight is no more harsh than Heaven's bliss,
If those in Heaven know of, and are grieved
By, the afflictions felt in the abyss
(Which may explain why Origen believed
That all, including Satan, at the end
Would find salvation and why Purgatory
Was first devised). But how can life extend
Beyond itself and yet not know the story
Of its own being? Disembodied souls

Assembled anywhere are hard enough
To comprehend for those whom flesh makes whole:
Without a brain and all the other stuff
That makes a body and without a past,
A soul is but a sigh in a gale's blast.

6

A soul is but a sigh in a gale's blast,
Invisible and too ephemeral
To matter if indeed it does exist.
Who, contemplating the material
By which we live, has failed to think this thought?
And if a soul does nothing but return,
Inert, to God, this thought seems—does it not?—
Most likely true. Whereas, if souls that burn
In Hell (if that's what souls there do) retain
Their human consciousness, one might elect
To go there and be stoic about pain.
Might or might not. The human intellect
Grasps less than it imagines, but mere rest
Is not fit contemplation for the blessed.

7

Is not fit contemplation for the blessed
To be with God and leave the rest to Him,
Above all, leave those questions unaddressed

No mind will ever answer? Minds grow dim;
I watched my mother's fade as mine will too;
She and the "coloured ladies" are long dead.
Yet minds were made to sort out false from true
And, where the sorting is inhibited,
To speculate, and speculations lead
To unmapped worlds. My mother's voice I hear
Call out, "You're in her way. Go out and weed
The garden." "No, I'm not," I persevere.
"A boy should mind his mama," sadly drawls
Our coloured lady as my mother calls.

Patricia Callan

Ruth's Work

"Meet friends? Go out? I don't see the need.
Solitude and I are pals," she said,
Firm and unmoved, yet oddly freed
By a severe new void around her bed.
She covered, then pushed her art against the wall,
Tossed out her work as one would kitchen waste.
"It was a phase, not worthy of recall —
Trivial sketches, easily replaced."

Still, there was one piece she hadn't shown,
A simply crafted loop with one slip knot;
As in the past, her work was done alone.
No critic could dismiss this objet d'art.
Displayed above a knocked down antique chair,
Ruth's body hung with grim artistic flair.

Michael Cantor

The Disappearance

There were no kids, the dogs are dead, and we're
completely out of touch. Old friends lived near,
and now or then I'd get a call and hear
that one had seen her, sitting in the rear
at some designer's show, or sipping kir
with groups of those young men who just appear
at every function, slim and cavalier,
and that she still looked good — but slightly queer,
and was not aging well — and I would fear
that she had asked for me. But year by year
my thoughts and interests moved from there to here.
The friends are gone — no longer volunteer
small updates on her sightings. Would a tear
or two in private now be real — or insincere?

Michael Cantor

Japanese for Beginners: Ronin

A *ronin* is a samurai without
a lord; a hired sword who boldly slaps
his sandals down the misted paths of sharp
Shikohu hills; and those he kills he knows

from their supporting roles in other blood-
soaked Kurosawa epic films: a priest,
a beggar monk, a warrior, a drunk—
one time he slew a *Daimyo* with one stroke,

fought bodyguards and courtiers—all slashed,
sent reeling, blind, through sun-bleached graveled
    courts,
to crash through *shojii* screens and flimsy walls
and die; their crimson handprints still alive

on swaying, spattered scrolls—then helped them up,
pulled out a smoke from deep kimono sleeves,
swept back his swords and joined the Daimyo's crew
at Toho's commissary buffet lunch:

a pleasant bunch—thieves, peasants, courtesans,
stout farmers, archers, artisans and such—
all ronins there, in service of the small
age-beaten Lord in glasses and beret

who would quite soon complete his duel, his film,
his life — die too — the players left again
to slouch from inn to inn; to roam the land
without a lord, without a truth: *ronin.*

Michael Cantor

Poem Noir

The trendy shades obscure the fact that she
is sixty. Her second husband, ninety-two,
is dying, inch-by-inch, beside the blue-
green tile Miami condo pool that he
is carried down to every day by two
Jamaican nurses, who agree that he,
betrayed by piss and prostate, wishes she
would simply let him be. Her *Gauloise* blue
silk scarf, the blonde and silver chignon she
affects, accent the tableau of the two
evading winter, hoping winter kills.
Fixed in the pose she sees to it that he
has shade, sighs to a friend in lighter blue,
"When my time comes, I have these little pills."

Michael Cantor

The Wind Rides a Harley

The Wind once rode a big, black, bad-ass Hawg,
a twisted blue bandanna on his head:
tattooed and sleeveless; lean, mean junkyard dog.

Now every flaming-asshole-walking-dead
executive has got hisself a bike:
middle-aged accountants dress alike
in stiff new leather gear, with *HARLEY* splashed
across their backs. The Wind stays home. Unwed,
alone, he surfs the net for porn instead
of cruising roads; eats Sugar Corn Pops stashed
beneath the bed; or sits and smokes his dope.

He thinks to buy some sneakers, join a group
that walks most mornings at the mall. He'll cope,
he says, and opens up a can of soup.

Michael Cantor

The Young Men in Their Beauty

There by the walls of Ilium
the young men in their beauty keep
graves deep in the alien soil
they hated and they conquered.
                —Aeschylus, The Orestia

The perfect children play lacrosse on beaten fields:
resplendent, gold on green; one flourishes the ball—
net-slung, dead white—as if to rally swords and shields
to heed an ancient call to arms and give their all

    against a scheming foe. But, see, the group that masses
    on a farther hill is tall, long-muscled, darker;
    defiantly the Iroquois make darting passes,
    hooting, clubbing; ash on flesh and gravel starker

than a referee's whistle. The favored children swarm
across an April carpet, sprinting, sticks on high;
the young men in their beauty revel, safe from harm,
and fill the sun-struck day with cries that amplify

    and echo between Mayan walls. Rude shadows cling
    to Chichen Itza courts as bone and skin meet skin
    and blood stains stone. A ball invades a chiseled ring
    set on a wall; and now the end-game shall begin

to play on beaten fields: *a bowl of hammered gold,*
a hard black knife, the children perfect, bright and bold.

Bill Coyle

Anima

One of those dismal, end-of autumn nights
I came around a bend and saw her there,
standing beside the road as though my lights
had conjured her from dark, rain-ridden air.
Twenty years old at most, slender, frail,
she stood with shoulders hunched against the rain,
her black hair pulled back in a pony tail,
her face a mask of disbelief and pain.
Poor soul... I knew exactly who she was
and thought of stopping there to help her when
she vanished suddenly, no doubt because
she knew I doubted she had ever been
anything more than my imaginings
projected on a darkened world of things.

Bill Coyle

_____

The God of this World to his Prophet

Go to the prosperous city,
for I have taken pity

on its inhabitants,
who drink and feast and dance

all night in lighted halls
yet know their bacchanals

lead nowhere in the end.
Go to them, now, commend,

to those with ears to hear,
a lifestyle more austere.

Tell all my children tired
of happiness desired

and never had that there
is solace in despair.

Say there is consolation
in ruins and ruination

beneath a harvest moon
that is itself a ruin,

comfort, however cold,
in grievances recalled

beside a fire dying
from lack of love and trying.

Bill Coyle

Leave Taking

i.m. Sten Söderström

The dead, we say, are the departed. They
pass on, they pass away, they leave behind
family, friends, the whole of humankind —
They have gone on before. Or so we say.

But could it be the opposite is true?
Now, as I stand here in the graveled drive
at moonrise, unaccountably alive,
I have the sense that it is we, not you,

who are departing, spun at breakneck speed
through space and time, while you stay where you are —
intimate of dark matter and bright star —
and watch the brilliant, faithless world recede.

The Magic Circle

1. Autumn

Early this morning I glanced out the window
and saw her underneath the maple tree.
She was as pale as that white gown of hers.
Hard to believe it's been a year already.
I waved. She turned away, paused for a moment,
then walked into the mist that marked the border
between my backyard and what lay beyond.
Proserpine, I called, but she was gone.
I am convinced that this was Proserpine
and not, as Mrs. Grandison maintains,
some nut escaped from the state hospital.
All Hallow E'en approaches. Skeletons
hang from the trees along my street and ghosts,
emboldened, haunt the front yards in broad daylight.

2. Winter

The swallows sleep beneath the river ice.
The salamanders whisper in the fire.
Hermes Trismestigus' new work is open
at one of its obscurer passages,
of which there are intolerably many.
I take a break to watch the local news.

Toward midnight, I collect my charts and go
to make my nightly survey of the heavens.
Mercifully they're still there. One of the saddest
developments I've witnessed in my time
has been astrology's decline from science
to fortune telling of the basest sort,
its long eclipse by disciplines that measure
not meaning, now, but distance, size and mass…
As if mere matter mattered in itself.

3. Spring

Bears wake from their long hibernation, now,
hirsute initiates with tales to tell
to those with ears to listen. Proserpine
returns as well, and Christ. And may not I?
The budding trees and the returning birds
figure the transmigration of the soul
so beautifully I wish that I could die
and see the world again through infant eyes.
I intimate these things to Ed, my mailman,
who nods politely. Ed is not about
to jeopardize his Christmas tip (last year
an old tin can transmuted into gold)
regardless how much of a character
he and the other villagers may think me.

4. Summer

Little did I know when I concocted
my potion that, although one may stop time,
it is impossible to turn it back.
Youth, they say, is wasted on the young.
Perhaps I'll have a tee-shirt made that reads,
Eternal life is wasted on the old.
And yet the world is no less beautiful.
Toward evening dew collects upon the lawn,
rising again as fireflies. Above
the white New England church a flock of swallows
copies a Greek text out in Arabic,
and in the maple trees a light breeze stirs,
sounding for all the world like water falling
distantly off the edges of the world.

The Moons of Earth

Earth, despite all the astronomers say, has not one
  moon but many.
All save the one called the Moon are inhabited, all
  have distinctive,
frankly fantastical climates and landscapes. Initiates
  know this,
meteorologists, farmers, sportsmen and almanac
  keepers
know what was once, in the antediluvian world,
  common knowledge.
They have conspired for six thousand years, now, to
  keep it a secret,
fearing that we, if we knew of inhabited worlds in
  near orbit,
might be so taken with them we'd neglect our
  terrestrial business.
And they are right. Having unearthed their secret
  I've found myself growing
arrogant, distant, bored with the everyday details
  of living,
pale and exhausted from gazing all night at the
  heavens. Oh stranger,
stranger whom I, both by chance and design,

entrust with the secret,
do not take lightly my warning; do not believe for a
    moment
you can believe in such things without gradually
    growing inhuman.
Think of the Harvest Moon, patchworked with
    wheatfields, orchards and vineyards;
think of the Hunter's Moon, teeming with prey
    unafraid of the arrow;
think of the Hunger Moon, peopled by figures
    from Giacometti;
think of the Flower Moon, the Ice Moon, the
    Strawberry Moon and the others.
You, if you ever return to your life, will return as a
    stranger.

Bill Coyle

Tjelvars Grav
Gotland, Sweden

It is a chilly day in late December.
The ground is dusted lightly over with snow.
The sun goes down at three, casting a glow
that freezes each particular in amber.
We shiver while we watch the last light go.

We note the sounds of passing traffic, brief
sighs, like the wind, brief stops of silence. Here,
just off the road a bit, where the trees clear,
a stone ship built to ply the afterlife
weathers the elements, year after year.

Here is the life-sized, dirt-floored hull of stones
so worn one half imagines it has been
to death's uncharted shore and back again.
Here, a plaque informs us, lay the bones
of an anonymous, seafaring man.

Tjelvar, the local legends call him, giving
to undistinguished bronze-age bones the name
of the apocryphal first man who came
to Gotland at the dawn of time. The living,
as always, are preoccupied with fame,

which is a kind of immortality,
though not, to judge from this, the concrete kind
Tjelvar (what else to call him?) had in mind.
Adrift on the unfathomable sea,
what was it he imagined he would find?

Lawrence saw vividly the new life's dawn.
Did Tjelvar see it, does he see it now,
staring intently from his stone ship's bow?
Or does he, in the dark, continue on,
drifting wherever wind and wave allow?

Or has he—I can hardly bear the thought—
dispassionately let his stone ship sink?
Did he slip under softly, did he drink
that dead sea's nothingness till he was not?
I am uncertain, finally, what to think.

I am unable, finally, to decide
if faith is more than one more way of trying
to make the factual less terrifying.
Tjelvar, if he ever lived, died.
A pair of gulls wheel overhead, crying.

Robert Crawford

French Braids

While one hand is content to touch, admire
A balanced, careful weave —preserve for viewing
The beauty and the boundaries of desire —
The other hand is busy at undoing.
The quiet hand counsels restraint; afraid
To wreck the composition of composure,
It's wary of destruction just for fun.
The other wants to slip between each braid,
To tease apart the strands, let run, spill over,
Release, unbind, what was so neatly done.
Your urgent kiss decides which hand is played.
A gentle pull brings argument to closure.
Surprised, my hands attempt to catch your hair:
It falls the way the rain lets go the air.

Robert Crawford

Power Failure

Groggy, at first, you think a bulb's burnt out.
But, the clock is off. The hum is gone.
An unfamiliar silence has returned.
Maybe it's just your room, but there's no water.
Maybe it's just the inn, but out the window,
Against the trees, the only light is the snow.
The valley down to Littleton is dark.
And so you wonder how far the failure goes:
This town; a few towns over; or did it start
Beyond the notch, spread all the way from Boston?
Because the silence seems so large, because
It's late at night, you wonder if there might
Have been a great catastrophe that changed
Everything on the other side of the mountains.
Though that would be an ugly, selfish thought,
Standing there looking out the window, and
Feeling the cold creep through the watery glass,
There is, engaged, a part of you—admit it!—
That wouldn't mind the starting all over again;
The desperate part of you that longs
For winter, and a covering of snow.

Robert Crawford

A Row of Stones

In those December storms that start as rain
But end as snow, I try to count the flakes
As they begin to fall. But it's in vain.
I lack the dedication that it takes
To be a census taker of the snow.
I'll be distracted, as the tumult breaks
Across the field, by a long gray narrow row
Of stones, a wall within a stand of birch:
A thousand stones at least, pried, grasped below,
Pulled up and piled. In this hard springtime work,
The greatest effort spent to make the wall
Was lifting each the first inch off the earth.
I know when things get high enough they fall;
I'm struck in wonder that they're raised at all.

Robert Crawford

Salisbury Cathedral

I know my eye is drawn to be inspired
By flight on flight of arched and buttressed stone,
And though the height meets what the eye required,
The heart is not impressed by this alone.
The place their lord gave them to build this church
Was bottomland, a home for fowl and fog,
And not, by all rights, firm enough to perch
The tons of marble resting on this bog.
Defying calculation and good sense,
The mass and burden of the task appalls.
While I could understand if it relents,
I feel in me for earth to hold these walls:
The single spire celebrates, above,
Their faith the ground could bear this weight of love.

Robert Crawford

The Swearing-in of Calvin Coolidge
Plymouth Notch, Vermont, 1923

Strange, the postman's loud, insistent knock
(The nearest phone, in town, two miles away)
Which roused them out of bed at one o'clock,
Tired from bringing in the August hay.
And stranger still, two telegrams they read
By lantern light: official ones, and both
With urgent news from Washington, that said,
"The President is dead. Please take the oath."
But in Vermont—where even summer skies
Can whisper that it's time to stack the wood,
And every breath on northern air implies
You're running out of days to do some good—
No one would be surprised, or think it odd
To see a man look up and say "So help me God."

Robert Crawford

Town Roads

At each town line the old town roads change names
To take the name of where you're coming from:
The Chester Road will bring you into Derry,
Derry Road ends at the Chester green.
Confusion wasn't built in by design —
The roads were laid like spokes on wagon wheels
To serve the farms that long ago moved west —
But this arrangement's hard on travelers
Who simply want to get from place to place.
What these towns need is a Copernicus
To tell them that the center lies without,
And agencies to legislate that roads
That run between them share a common name.
And yet, when sitting on the bench behind
Two cannons and a monument to boys
Who went, when asked, to save that wider world,
But never came back down these wrong-named roads,
I see the possibility: perhaps
The towns were right. All roads don't lead to Rome;
They do, however, radiate from home.

Robert Crawford

The Whole of It

This first hot day, under an apple tree,
I feel you as a single drop of sweat
That slips along the middle of my back,
Along my spine, and traces me upon
Some magic paper that could take a man
And make him known, in no particulars,
Just known — as a land for its geography,
But where no valley, town, or mountain could
Explain the whole of it. I know, and yet,
This one wet fingertip of yours could map
Exactly what I am, and what might be,
And make each blossom hum above my head.

Rhina P. Espaillat

Butchering

My mother's mother, toughened by the farm,
hardened by infants' burials, used a knife
and swung an axe as if her woman's arm
wielded a man's hard will. Inured to life
and death alike, "What ails you now?" she'd say
ungently to the sick. She fed them too,
roughly but well, and took the blood away —
and washed the dead, if there was that to do.
She told us children how the cows could sense
when their own calves were marked for butchering,
and how they lowed, their wordless eloquence
impossible to still with anything —
sweet clover, or her unremitting care.
She told it simply, but she faltered there.

Rhina P. Espaillat

Encounter

Under the dark leaves of a summer night
I met my father, dead these fourteen years;
no less whole flesh than I nor ghostly bright,
he seemed himself in that uncertain light:
we spoke of common things and shed no tears.

Having rehearsed the wish, I thought I knew
what words would heal the hurt of life gone wrong
over small failures, exorcise the long
regrets the dead still haunt; but words half true
had not the power of healing like a song.

Such as we were and had been and must be,
love or no love, we were at break of day;
and then my spectre vanished, leaving me
with everything and nothing yet to say,
nothing to do but live and walk away.

Rhina P. Espaillat

Hang Gliders

Look at them, cresting their silken tide,
riding an airy coil through waves of sun,
levitating above us where, afraid,
we squint and hug our bit of broken stone.
How must it feel, after the first sick
lift into nothing, to be held aloft
by nothing, leaning windward like a hawk?
But time will teach us that, since every craft
slips from its own command at last to tremble
free, as in the giddy wind of love
and undertow of loss we stumble
into wisdom, lapse to grace, give,
flow on the breath that speaks us, cease to know,
forget ourselves, become ourselves, let go.

Rhina P. Espaillat

Highway Apple Trees

Nobody seeds this harvest, it just grows,
miraculous, above old caps and cans.
These apples may be sweet. Nobody knows

if they were meant to ripen under those
slow summer clouds, cooled by their small green fans.
Nobody seeds this harvest, it just grows,

nodding assent to every wind that blows,
uselessly safe, far from our knives and pans.
These apples may be sweet. Nobody knows

what future orchards live in cores one throws
from glossy limousines or battered vans.
Nobody seeds this harvest; it just grows,

denied the gift of purpose we suppose
would give it worth, conferred by human hands.
These apples, maybe sweet (nobody knows)

soften and fall, as autumn comes and goes,
into a sleep well-earned as any man's.
Nobody seeds this harvest, it just grows.
These apples may be sweet. Nobody knows.

Rhina P. Espaillat

If You Ask Me

"If you ask me," said the snake, "this couple's doomed:
they started naked, not a thing to need,
a thing to wonder at, since orders boomed
over the speaker. Every day they weed
a little, see what's ripe and pluck it off,
eat this, no don't eat that. Now I'm not blind:
I see her fidget with her hair and cough
that nervous cough; she's bored out of her mind.
I see him gawk at birds and flap in vain;
then his blank eyes cloud over with the sky
and circle his estate, so green, so plain.
She's ripe to risk herself; they need to die;
unbanished, he's an ornament, a brute.
We're neighbors; I'll go visiting, with fruit."

Rhina P. Espaillat

My Cluttered House Accuses Me of Greed

My cluttered house accuses me of greed,
or at the very least the love of things,
how they seduce the eye, play to the hand,
pretend to speak for us. How shall I plead?
Guilty, guilty, and gladly! Take those wings
away, that halo: dressed for earth, I stand
convicted of no saintly taste at all
for spirit's leanness. No, I mean to fall,
heavy with sound and color, dense as clay,
into the rose and satin of old wood,
the kiss of wine still on my lip to say
this much I tasted once, and it was good.
Afterward, let my shadow find its way
to who knows what austere new neighborhood.

Rhina P. Espaillat

There is a Man

There is a man goes stumbling through this town,
his left side trembling as if struck by stroke
or palsy, maybe, and he wears a face
that says, "I want this," looking steady, down
where feet must totter straight. We never spoke,
I do not know him, but in all this place
nobody says so surely or so clear,
Desire is all there is to keep us here.

How easy—irresistible, for me—
in the ungainly shoes he drags with such
tenacity, to falter, to let be,
let go. Just once, I think, release your touch
on that hard substance, life, and you go free.
How wonderful to want it all that much.

Vignette

Andromache, one misty morning,
walking the city's crown of stones,
is startled by a cry whose warning
pierces the marrow of her bones.

The child beneath her heart is stirred,
turns in its groove as if to know
what augury without a word
intrudes where such calm waters flow.

The sentry, stolid at his post,
salutes Prince Hector's pretty wife.
He cannot know how, ghost by ghost,
she has relinquished death for life.

He wonders why she reads this place
as if it were a graven prayer,
as if Scamander's cursive pace
inscribed the sum of blessings there.

How blessed—she thinks—this plain, unhaunted,
where those I cherished never bled;
blessed, to be ordinary, wanted
by the good man who shares my bed.

The mist has cleared; far off and pale,
the cry she heard takes form at last:
only a gull, circling a sail
approaching neither slow nor fast.

Rhina P. Espaillat

Weighing In

What the scale tells you is how much the earth
has missed you, body, how it wants you back
again after you leave it to go forth

into the light. Do you remember how
earth hardly noticed you then? Others would rock
you in their arms, warm in the flow

that fed you, coaxed you upright. Then earth began
to claim you with spots and fevers, began to lick
at you with a bruised knee, a bloody shin,

and finally to stroke you, body, drumming
intimate coded messages through music
you danced to unawares, there in your dreaming

and your poems and your obedient blood.
Body, how useful you became, how lucky,
heavy with news and breakage, rich, and sad,

sometimes, imagining that greedy zero
you must have been, that promising empty sack
of possibilities, never-to-come tomorrow.

But look at you now, body, soft old shoe
that love wears when it's stirring, look down, look
how earth wants what you weigh, needs what you know.

Lois Frankenberger

_____

Kaddish

I never really saw a body bag
until they took my mother out in one—
after she died at home in her sleep only
one year short of her 100th year—with my sister,
me, one trained nurse and one young companion
standing by, away from the bedroom, backs turned
to the strangers who worked without
a sound until *zip, zip, zip,* and she was ready.
A bolt of deep red, heavy duty nylon
with a double set of carrying straps
hanging from the hands of the two men
passed quietly beyond us
as if the bundle were ten feet long
and we slipped into prayer to break the silence.
Yisgadal v'yiskadash I whispered, wondering
if my mother would approve
of this ceremonial gesture
shmey rabbah I chanted, thinking
red was not my mother's favorite color
b'alma div ra hu, remembering
her lust for the beautiful life
and her face disfigured by cancer
v'imroo ah'main, knowing

she was finally going home
to lie next to my father
dressed to perfection in
pure white linen.
She always loved linen —
it should only not wrinkle.

Midge Goldberg

The Fish

"But what about the fish?" my daughter asks.
We're reading, for a bedtime story, Noah,
Who's busy with at least a million tasks
Preparing place for sheep, flamingo, boa,
But there's no mention of the fish. I say,
 "That's true; of course, they wouldn't care about
A flood—in fact, they'd have more room that way,"
But why did God decide to leave them out?
Were they unsullied more than beast or bird?
Forgotten? Was it too hard to make disaster
Really work for everyone? No word
On this. They got no promises or master,
Nothing they did not need, no watery bow.
Untouched by God, the fish stayed safe below.

Midge Goldberg

The Flume Ride

Your arms slide around my waist, and we are going,
and I am pressed full length back into you.
We click and rock heavenward only knowing
the outline of the way but not the view,
the feel of every curve, turning and twisting.
Our fingers intertwine, and gravity
falls before us, leaving us resisting
in a well of weightlessness, then we

are dropping, through loops and lesser hills
of rapids run to overspills,
locked and tumbling together, falling
like eagles plummeting, calling,
until the boat slows, and we are there.
Your fingers comb the water from my hair.

Midge Goldberg

Hometown Bars—
If I Went Back

I'd talk to the girl with auburn hair
next to the mirrored barroom wall:
what made me leave, what kept her there,

eyes of green, skin so fair,
queen of every high school ball.
I'd talk to the girl with auburn hair,

remember how, with one slow stare,
she got the boys to come and call.
I had to leave, and she stayed there,

to marry young, each day aware
of the always-watchful eyes of all.
She was "the girl with auburn hair,"

and I was not. I took the spare
leftover names—the smart one, small—
and left: no one could keep me there.

But still I sit in a vacant chair
next to the mirrored barroom wall.
The green-eyed girl, the auburn hair—
what we believed would keep us there.

Midge Goldberg

On Air

"We had our wedding on the radio.
Yeah, we won this contest where you called in
to answer things about each other—jeez,
I could have killed Mike when he didn't know
my high school boyfriend's name. They all played hockey
together for Saint Mary's—and he forgot!
The questions they asked me were really dumb—
who'd he want to be? How the heck should I know?
But it was right after the Super Bowl,
that year the Pats won (what a party—I
got wicked smashed). I figured he'd say Tom,
uh, what's his name, their quarterback—the cute one.
So, yeah, we won, 'cause I got that one right.
And then the prize was, they paid for the whole
friggin' wedding at Casa di Fior—
that place up Route 1 by the mini-golf,
(it's wicked expensive there; I checked it out) —
a honeymoon vacation in Aruba,
and then they put the whole thing on the air
(the wedding, not the honeymoon—oh my God!).
The vows and everything! I think my ma
was kind of sad we didn't have a priest.
They brought their own JP (a Catholic one—

he took one look at ma and Aunt Therese
and did a quick Our Father over the cake—
they felt a little better after that).
Those DJ guys, and Lila in the Morning,
they were there. It was an awesome party.
Even Uncle Donny said so, and he
should know, he caters weddings all the time.
When I got back, people I didn't know
at work would come right up to me and say,
'Hey, I heard your wedding on the air.'
That was cool. Like I was famous maybe.
Like Madonna."

Midge Goldberg

Town Parade

I sit on the curb and watch them marching, feel
that raw spot open like a just-scraped knee.
The school band wears plain pants and shirts—where are
the uniforms we wore in junior high?
They pass: the crooked lines, the fat flag girls;
drum majors lead the band with empty hands.
Where is the gleaming scepter, coveted
like gold? The whistle, hat, those gloves that slashed
the air, acknowledged—yes, to be acknowledged.
Or sequined bathing suits of majorettes:
custom-made, with boots, tiara, beauty.
You'd give up music to be one of those girls.
They were the gods, the queens, our tailored hell.
They're missing here today—it's just as well.

A. M. Juster

Cancer Prayer

Dear Lord,
        Please flood her nerves with sedatives
and keep her strong enough to crack a smile
so disbelieving friends and relatives
can temporarily sustain denial.

Please smite that intern in oncology
who craves approval from department heads.

Please ease her urge to vomit; let there be
kind but flirtatious men in nearby beds.

Given her hair, consider amnesty
for sins of vanity; make mirrors vanish.

Surround her with forgiving family
and nurses not too numb to cry. Please banish
trite consolations; take her in one swift
and gentle motion as your final gift.

A. M. Juster

Letter to Auden

Uh, Wystan?
> Please forgive my arrogance;
> You know how most Americans impose.
Your chat with Byron gave me confidence
> That your Platonic ghost would not oppose
> Some verse disturbing you from your repose.
Besides, there's time to kill now that the Lord
Has silenced Merrill and his ouija board.

Or do you pine for peace in Paradise,
> Besieged by every half-baked psychic hack
Intent on mining gems from your advice?
> With me, please don't insist on writing back
> Unless you can't resist some biting crack.
I also recognize that I had better
Keep my remarks far shorter than your *Letter.*

Indeed, I'll need some substantial guile and nerve
> To try to emulate your bracing pace.
At twenty-nine, your lines had style and verve;
> My work at thirty-nine seems commonplace
> And foreordained to sink without a trace.
In any case, I do not hold out hope
Of sharing space with you or spiteful Pope.

A partial consolation on bad days
        Is no contemporary can compete
With you at all. Downtrodden MFA's
        Denounce the Audenesque as obsolete
        Oppression by your dead-white-male elite,
But then they go on to become depressed
Because there's nothing left to be confessed.

Only a few eccentrics still support
        Those poets who can scan lines properly.
However, I'm delighted to report
        That you became a hot pop property
        When *Four Weddings* exhumed your poetry.
You would have been amused to see its star
Arrested with a hooker in his car

But shocked that we remain so schizophrenic.
        Our sordid scandals rarely stay concealed
Although we want things guiltless and hygienic.
        Gay Studies has developed as a field
        In which great writers' lovers are revealed;
You lose some points for marrying a Mann
And your diversity of goings-on.

As your long-suffering but faithful fan,
        I must disclose you missed the NEA,
The disco era, Gump and daily bran.

In short, you would assess the present day
As drearily debased and déclassé.
Well, Wystan, this is all that I can muster.
Give my regards to Byron.

Fondly,
Juster

A. M. Juster

Los Periquitos

for Rhina Espaillat

The parakeets of Brooklyn beat the cold
by building homes near incidental heat.
They hunt for laundry vents, the gaps in old
facades, or humming coils above the street,
then stake their fragile claims with twigs and scraps
they take from roofs and sidewalks. Joyously,
they mate in maple trees, and dodge the traps
of easy birdseed and security.

Though this unlikely flock delighted fans,
consultants argued it would not survive.
They later pushed eradication plans—
supposedly so native breeds could thrive.
We should have known these studies were a waste,
for true New Yorkers cannot be displaced.

A. M. Juster

Moscow Zoo

We saw the mass grave at the Moscow Zoo.
A sullen man dug up a human skull
Then held it high for journalists to view.
Forensic specialists arrived to cull
Remains and clues from this forgotten plot
On which the zoo still plans to cage a bear.
The experts guessed these prisoners were shot
For special reasons; no one was aware
Of comparable scenes at urban sites.
No one knew if these bones belonged to spies,
Suspected Jews or zealous Trotskyites,
So none of us displayed the least surprise
When bureaucrats emerged from quiet cars
To hint this might have been the work of czars.

A. M. Juster

Note from Echo

Narcissus, I no longer haunt the canyons
and the crypts. I thrive and multiply;
uncounted daughters are my new companions.

We are the voicemail's ponderous reply
to the computers making random calls.
We are the Muzak in the empty malls,
the laugh track on the reruns late at night,
the distant siren's chilling lullaby,
the steady chirp of things that simplify
their scheduled lives. You know I could recite
more, but you never cared for my recitals.

I do not miss you, do not need you here —
I can repeat the words of your disciples
telling lovers what they need to hear.

A. M. Juster

Visions of the Serengeti

When Mutual of Omaha supported
nature shows, they spared us sex and gore.
We stared as peacocks preened and rhinos courted,
then later saw the litters—nothing more.
The mother wombats would protect their young
(just as insurance agents do for you)
and Marlon would relax while Jim's life hung
in balance, for their dartgun's aim was true.

I watch new nature shows now with my spaniel.
She wags her tail as jackals disembowel
the wildebeest of The Discovery Channel,
then warns off flapping vultures with a growl.
Her rapture grows until the carnage stops,
then she considers me, and licks her chops.

Merrill Kaitz

Blue Antelope Elegy

"Just east of Capetown..., a Boer huntsman shot the very last blaauwbok, or blue antelope... completing the first extinction of a large-bodied mammalian species in historic times... Most agree on a terminus of 1799."
　　　　　　　　—S. J. Gould, <u>Natural History</u>, May, 1994

1.

How blue was the blue
antelope? Who
can remember yesterday
morning's sky?

Too ethereal for the earthly veldt
the skittish blaubok ducked into the bush
and never grazed again. No benefit accrued
to the blaubok just for being blue.

2.

A blaubok brouhaha broke out
among the mammalologists.
Which patch of skin, which skeleton defined
the ruminant's rare soul?

Who cared this much for blaubok
when it lived?
Who worried
over blaubok's body then?

3.

Blind shepherds and the grazing herd
crowded the blaubok out.
Huntsmen harvested their azure coats
and fed their sinew to the thoughtless dogs.

"I may truly say," wrote Kolb,
"that this animal appeared
especially beautiful because its hair
is so much like the color of the sky."

The thrifty economy of the human spirit
discovered how to carve the sky
and wear it
and feed the clouds to hounds.

4.

It dartled between bush and grass,
a small, rare delicate noble thing
of unselfconscious azure, a small patch
of sky made mammal for a moment only.

A bluebacked blaubok
mounts his fragile ewe.
After her sweet bleats
the final tupping ends.

The last sticky kid
descends from womb to light
to skitter through underbrush alone
till night.

Don Kimball

Deer in a Craft Shop

It might have been the early morning light
that caught her eye, while she dashed down a one-
way street that night, persuading her to cross
a wide divide —where, later in the day,
she would've had to wobble in the sun
for speeding cars to stop, before she'd dare
to trot the crosswalk. Now, beguiled by some
random need, she strides the four-lane street,
smashing through glitter into shards of glass,
and leaping down, not onto moss or leaves,
but the astonished sales floor. Mouths agape,
the city road crew stand outside and watch,
while the whitetail doe negotiates
a labyrinth of narrow aisles. "Oh, no—
there goes another vase!" yells one of them.
She stops behind a shiny case, as if
gazing with longing at a silver bracelet,
appraising the delicacy of her plight,
when light, that winking light, bewilders her,
invites her back to thrash some inner darkness,
where she attempts to vault a jeweler's bench
and leaps, with a shatter of window panes,
into the blinding glare —a wounded doe
falling two stories to a parking lot,
hobbling a trail of blood and broken vases.

Don Kimball

Milk Can

As if she's heard intruders at the door,
but would not trust the lock to keep her safe,
should they come bursting in—who knows what for—
the widow, clutching at her flannel robe,
takes hold of an old milk can—like her kitchen
a handy catch-all; this object that cannot
object to her unladylike abuse—
tilts it back and slowly wheels it sideways
(as she once saw her husband deal with barrels),
steers it through a narrow passageway,
between a closet, some unforgiving stairs,
clear to the entry, where she lets it go,
wedges it tight against the door, says, *There!*—
as if she's finally got that big old house,
with all its rooms, secured against desire;
as if, by blocking doors, she's doused the fire.

Elaine Kimball

Burying Burley

They scattered Burley in the sea today—
Just Buddy and the guy that buys the fish;
Took him in Buddy's boat to Ipswich Bay
To the urchin beds. It was Burley's wish
To go where they went every blessed day
And float to bottom where the action is.

An educated man, handsome and tall,
A businessman with plenty set aside,
Burley would not give up the alcohol.
His wife had left him when he hardly tried.
His married daughter didn't even call.
When he was diagnosed, nobody cried.

The women clucked and disapproved of him,
To disregard his health the way he did.
Tender work was difficult and grim,
And Buddy was a drunken, vulgar kid.
Burley felt his substance growing slim—
A rotted rope unravelled by a fid.

It was Burley's plan to drink himself to death
With a pal or two, a boat, a job to do;

To live each day with whiskey on his breath;
To have a captain and to be a crew.
To mix himself with water when he left
In a world that lunges for its food.

This morning started out like any day,
Coffee at Buddy's with a coffin nail.
They brought out Burley's mug for old times' sake.
They filled his flask with bourbon, best of pail,
Took the cap he wore since chemo every day,
The old full-billed cap shiny with fish scales.

They scattered Burley in the sea today,
Just like he wanted, right over the side.
The whiskey, an anchor, plunged into the Bay;
His cap, a small craft, drifted off with the tide.
Buddy's not reckless, despite what they say,
But he will dive solo now Burley's died.

Elaine Kimball

Santi, the Communist Shoemaker

Mr. Santi, the card-carrying Communist shoemaker,
Had a shop on Washington down by the post office
    building,
Across from Jake's Bar with the jars of pickled eggs
    and kielbasa
Right next to May's News, where they sold penny candy
    and gum
With the daily newspaper, and handed out gossip for free.
Weekly cell meetings went on in the back of Santi's
    shoe shop,
And May knew who went to those meetings every
    Wednesday night,
But she would never tell because it was nobody's
    business.

It was just after the second war that did not end all wars,
When no one believed there would be plenty of sugar
    and smokes,
And kept pouring condensed milk in their coffee and
    hoarded butts.
But in the toughest of times the children must have
    sturdy shoes.
Santi, the Communist shoemaker, fitted us twice a year —

Considered our summer-calloused soles and touched
  our dirty heels,
Expertly measured length and width, the distance
  from tongue to toe.
There was no discussion of style, because there was
  only one,

One heavy thick-soled style in brown leather with
  proper laces
And six months of extra room for unruly toes to grow in.
Money did not change hands; no delivery date was
  promised.
"Two weeks?" my mother asked. The Communist
  shoemaker nodded.
Then we would walk home, past Foster's Drugstore,
  a magical place
Where they squirted sweet bubbly drinks out of a
  rubber hose,
Piled ice cream and whipped cream and cherries into
  metal dishes,
And sold tortures like cod liver oil and tincture of
  iodine.

In two weeks the shoes would come, wrapped in
  butcher paper and string.
My little sister, who had no idea her shoes were ugly,
Would be as agitated as a pup and breathe in their
  smell,

And would say to all comers every day, "Smell my
   shoes." They did.
I wanted to shout "I want loafers!" but never did or
   would.
I smiled and said "Thank you" and tried never to
   look at my feet.
Just before I went to seventh grade, the dreaded
   junior high,
The inevitable shoes came. When I opened them up,
   they were red.

The year I left for college, it was penny loafers at last.
I spent my days in old libraries that smelled like
   sturdy shoes,
My head redolent with ideologies sniffed and
   dismissed,
Yet I continue to ponder the irony of red shoes.
The shoemaker never had wife or child; May told me
   he died.
If I could find his grave, I would not leave him a
   blatant rose
Or plant a reeking hyacinth for the sake of his sere
   soul,
But I would sickle the weeds on his grave. I owe him
   that much.

Len Krisak

Birds from Afar

Against what's left of one day's light,
They rise, cleaving the cold white air
As if in leaving on this flight
They thought they might not get somewhere.
And yet their soaring seems so blind,
As dozens wheel back, swoop, and swerve,
    Like chaff that's changed its mind,
    Or love that's lost its nerve.

Len Krisak

Common

Even my enemies by day
        By night will dream —
Impossible as it must seem
        That we should share that way.
This man spewing in my face;
That woman cocked to throw her drink:
        All end up in a place
        Where none may think.

All lie down under cover of
        The darkness shared
By those for whom we never cared
        And those we cannot love.
Deep down my mortal equal lies,
Unconscious in the sleep that knows
        No way to recognize
        That we are foes.

And come that other sleep we call
        A sleep, what then?
Shall I share that with other men
        I cannot bear at all?
Before I dream, I ponder this,
Perhaps preparing to forgive
        Those souls I would not miss.
        I let them live.

Len Krisak

Constance Marvin

She loved the stage, Debate and Speech, and—most
Of all—Miss Simpson, miles away in gym.
We seldom wondered why there seemed no "him"
At her periphery. Her closet closed,
Miss Marvin concentrated on each kid,
That we might learn to sway some luncheon crowd
Or "sell" the Senior Play. Her heart lay hid,
Who taught that love you could not speak out loud
Could still be love; that still those girls and boys
Might safely con phonetic alphabets
And plummy diction, proper posture, poise.
No doubt she thought those were the only debts
We'd ever owe her. Oh, how she was wrong;
This draft I write out now took far too long.

Len Krisak

Day-Schoolers on a Walk

The word *bemused* (I mean the sense
It used to have) comes first to mind.
They wind their way in innocence,
It seems, the few school ties that bind
Them coiled around their coats — a rope
Of cheerful yellow braids. Each looks
Up, off, and back, though what they hope
To see, this chain gang's toddler-crooks,
Is anybody's guess. They press
Ahead in spaced-out, crooked file,
To get to where their governess
Will lead them on, a crocodile
Of kindergartners snaking down
The pavement, bound for where they're bound.

Len Krisak

Mrs. Henley

Way back when Dinah Shore still roamed the earth
(And ruled its airwaves), Mrs. Henley taught
Us English Lit for all that she was worth.
As crimped and banged as Mamie, auburn-tressed
And prone to smiles, she amplified each thought
By recourse to an earnest lesson plan
She cradled to her primly tailored breast.
"'And justify the ways of God to men.'
Now, Leonard, what did Milton mean by that?"
A glance, a check beside a question mark,
Then on to thirty years of those who sat
Where I had sat and caught her modest spark.
Methodical and sure of every word,
She spoke her spinster's love until I heard.

Len Krisak

On Finishing a Translation of *Ovid's* Amores

And on this day ten short of Valentine's,
I set my pen down, done with *Loves* at last.
Now free from these not-quite-three-thousand lines,
I put all puerile pimping in the past,
Along with *pudor, puer,* and *puellae.*
Now there will be no sex unless I choose,
And only English show, not Latin tell. I
Will wait to hear the breathing of the Muse,
Heavy or shallow. Following her lead,
Perhaps then I will write my own true verse,
Thanking my lucky stars that I've been freed
To crank out sonnets on how nothing's worse
Than being chained to someone else's soul.
Perhaps such poems wait. Let's hope they're droll.

Len Krisak

Plumbing Emergency

Frantic as waters rise,
He finds the hidden, seized-up valve and twists —
An act that hardly buys
Him time to think,
But memory resists:
Where has she stashed that number?
"Too soon to slash the wrists,"
He hears his antic brain advise.
Racing from sink
To phone, riffling the seldom-thumbed-through wad
Of business cards that hides a plumber,
He hauls up short. Oh, God.

Deep in that pristine stack
Of cheaply-lettered print raised in relief:
Her lover, ten years back.
The dated snap
Makes one of them a thief.
He sees that — somehow — clearly,
But what has come to grief?
His trust in her? Or just its lack?
Cold waters slap:
Wrenched, he knows he has a call to make,
And sees that someone will pay dearly.
His phone hand starts to shake.

Len Krisak

_____

A Version of Akhmatova

—from her book Evening, *1910*

The three things that he loved the most
Were Juno's bird, old New World maps,
    And litanies at dusk.
    But raspberry jam on toast,
    Or little kids who cried,
A nervous woman in relapse,
And he became a basilisk.
    And I became his bride.

Len Krisak

What of the Night?

How precious little did I even sense
The burden of our safety that he bore
Who rattled first the back and then front door?
What could I know of harm thought so immense
And bodiless? It was an inside job,
Guarding the one house he was watchman of,
Trying first one and then another knob,
That we might sleep securely locked in love.
Now as I mimic what I watched him do,
Testing our bolts each night, just to be sure,
Do I drift off the least bit more secure
Than fifty years ago? Can that be true?
Then when he's townsman of the stillest town,
Who will I be to set his burden down?

Michele Leavitt

Charm School

Of course, it was unbearable
To me, as I was awkwardly
Between the flat, intractable
Self that's called a child, and the curvy
Mystery of a woman's need
To please. My mother paid for me
To go. We were taught about nice looks
And modest posture, how to feed
Our surfaces with creams, how books
Could give us wrinkles, how to cope
With rudeness and direct attack
Submissively. And now, friends hope
My mother got her money back.

Michele Leavitt

Ladies Night

*"Hold a pebble in your mouth to reduce
the sensation of thirst."*
—Survival tip

It started in a washed-up biker bar,
First letting Judy, former puffer-queen
And party-girl for Angels, brag on me,
Her college girl. The bikers lined up shots
And beers for me. I thought that I could take
The things I wanted from that world and walk
On whole to what I thought was next. The bar
Was full of idle whores who'd doped themselves
Together, piece by piece, so they could give
Up any piece they chose to later on.
Who did I think I was? They jumped me on
The sidewalk, snarled their hands around my hair,
My imitation pearls, as if these were
Just ropes to pull me to the leveled ground.
The pearls spilled off into the gutter, small
White mice escaping sudden light. The girls
Got bored and went back in the bar, left me
To limp away, to leave a trail of hair
Along the bricks. What did I give up first,
To get the things I craved? This story rolls
Just like a pearl inside my mouth. It clicks
Against my teeth, against all kinds of thirst.

Michele Leavitt

Unspent

What happens to a love that's isn't spent,
That's merely saved? Poor misers hoard their gold
As if such spending's an impediment
To virtue's gate, but unspent love will fold
Up like a fan, discreetly sleeved, will vow
To hide, and still smell faintly like a blood-
Red wine that's out of reach, that will not drown
Your tongue, that will not drag you through the mud
Of consequence, the censure of your town,
Or through the gates of bliss. Enjoy it now—
The virtue you collect from each refusal,
The secret thrill you sense with each perusal
Of your trove—this love that isn't spent.
You cannot take it with you—or repent.

Nancy Bailey Miller

Grief

The woman lost her son, and now her hat
is missing. Messages on all the Chapel
phones. Her favorite hat, the Borsalino
cloche, perhaps we'll find it underneath
a pew or couch in Baldwin Cloister. She
looked everywhere that day.
                                    Today
another message on the phone. The hat
was black, her signature, crushed velvet;
maybe someone picked it up and thought
it was a scarf.

Nancy Bailey Miller

Noah's Wife

Weeks ago I noticed clouds' dark festering.
He kept muttering had I heard of cubits.

Rain. A first plump drop on my dry path
and then another. Did he notice gulls

this morning so far inland? Does he smell
the camel? No. He's nailing now. He's busy.

Beyond my folded tent-flap, rivulets digging
channels; two by two the salamanders

turn to parrot fish. Two rabbits pause,
a pair of geese, two deer. It's soaking, teeming,

water rushing, splatting. Ankle deep,
I wade alone. Alone, with unsure footing.

Currents swirl like dervish dancers, sitar
driven. Finally here's the splintery plank

to board. He's busy, covered. One by one
I climb—I climb alone to save myself.

James Najarian

Armenian Lesson

with refrains from Gulian's Armenian Grammar, 1904

Aloud, one grants its gutturals to the air:
Intimate, prolific hard h's and j's,
Sounds for the kitchen, meant to bear
Advice, instruction, succor, and homilies:
The quieter a life, the happier it is.

On paper, its trampled circles, squat wings,
And curlicued ladles can only convey
Spoken embroidery—a collection of things
You seldom have occasion to say:
The Count and Countess are in York today;

Coachman, Gooseberry, or *Sealing-wax.*
The grammarian carefully arranges the letters
In sample sentences whose slight effects
Predict none of this country's future disasters:
Each boy has received seven piastres.

We are expecting too much from this tongue—
More than thirty-eight letters can give.
No living language could ever be strong
Enough for those it could not save.
The Turkish soldiers are very brave.

James Najarian

Goat Song

You never had just one. We had forty,
And no one ever went without a name;
To this day, in my family's photo albums
The people have been butted out by goats:
'There's Bippy,' we cry out, 'There's Charmian.'
In general they had attractive names
That you would hesitate to give your daughter:
Candy, Ceffie, Bambi, Serenade —
Or sometimes a descriptive sobriquet:
Velveeta, for a chubby orange doe,
Regina, for her royal roman nose,
Frisbee, for one who leapt all fences, teaching
A trip of young does how to follow her.

In their eyes, everything was ready to be tasted.
They thrived on poison ivy, stinging nettle,
Corn stubble, honeysuckle, chickweed, bark.
They would gnaw holes in your sweaters, gulp pages
Of a book. (One gobbled up a tarpaulin.)
They had selves without self-consciousness.
Their gestures celebrated their desires:
The teeth they showed off when they were content
Making them grin like happy, hairy gators.

How they would squat to pee, at any time
Completely unaware, as an example,
That they were watering your sneakers. How they
Would line up to be petted, then afterward
Your hands would be veneered with several layers
Of fragrant grime. Their ears, like flesh-lined felt.
Their constant rheumy burping. The shit-and-lemon
Cologne they carried on them. How they hated
Two things above all: being alone, and rain.
Most memorably, their eyes, which spun
In almost separate orbits. Their pupils
Opened horizontally, like trestles
Bestowing them a sideways Weltanschaung,
Exquisitely contrived for sabotage:
Feed bins to ransack, latches to undo,
Hayracks to get stuck in, pails to overturn.
They broke though fences, scorned electric wires,
Obliterated gardens. When you found them
They rubbed their heads on you for gratitude.

But goats live only six or seven years.
In our herd, they seemed to die unceasingly
Like heroines from nineteenth-century opera—
Of mysterious, long thought curable diseases;
'Milk Fever,' Abscess, Bloat, 'Flash Toxin.' Their deaths
Were harrowing; they moaned and knew their going,
And they exhausted us. My mother sold

The strongest, leaving two beloved does,
Our pets. The old goats home, we called it.

                                    Now
They cameo and gambol through my sleep
Gluttoning blissfully somewhere unreachable,
Or padding after me through fragrant hills.
I start up in my wide suburban bed,
Patting the mattress, hoping they are real,
And call the names that seem to be for strippers:
Candy, Ceffie, Bambi, Serenade,
Just as the names come out, I understand
Them decades—caprine generations—gone.
Leaving me only with a mild surmise:
That somewhere their uncountable-great grandkids
Are cramming their mouths with rose and thistle, breaking
Out of other pastures, with some other boy.

Mildred Nash

Hera, Elderly

Hera, wearing orthopedic shoes,
still struts. Her years are regal as antiques.
Age craves new travel, although avenues
grow inaccessible, the carriage weak.

"I want! I want!" the ancient peacock cries
as lustily as ever. Bones become
more disobedient than children, rise
reluctantly, threatening to succumb;
and yet volition never flags. Rage
at a failing body drives her on.

About desire she is never vague.
The list of things she'd do remains as long
at eighty as it was at eight and grows
ever more reckless as the years foreclose.

Mildred Nash

North Country Graveyard

Across the landscape lively walls of stone
each winter heave a slightly new direction —
as if the dead would strike out on their own

rather than rest in such a place alone
with twenty shades of granite jettisoned
across the landscape. The silent slabs of stone

could tell their winter tales against the blown
austerity of snow would someone listen —
but here the dead are strictly on their own.

The will to live seems sturdier than bone;
a restless air disturbs what's been undone.
Across the landscape growing rows of stone

stand as a tally of all those I've known
who've gone from breath to death's oblivion.
Each added death acquaints me with my own

and yet for all my fear and resignation,
for all my grief, for me death is not done.
Across the landscape walls of mocking stone
remind me no death kills me but my own.

Mildred Nash

Vineyard Conjuring

One thing calls another thing to mind,
and by these tricks of conjured memory
I lose myself in what I try to find.

Ocean. Oak Bluffs. The end of June. A blind
piano player. Misty drinks. I see
how one thing calls another thing to mind.

Words clustering in moonlight off behind
The Island House under a light-laced tree,
I lose myself in what I try to find.

Among the campground cottages entwined
with gingerbread and salt-air fantasy,
each thing calls another thing to mind.

Lantana. Lobster pots. A drifting line
of poetry unwritten, not to be.
I lose myself in everything I find

until the porches fill with dark, resigned
to end this lazy, late-night reverie.
Nothing at last calls anything to mind.
What have I lost? What had I hoped to find?

Karen Nelson

Flamenco Dancer

She wakes her two children
    who sleep with her in the family caverna.
Their father joined a gypsy caravan
    bound for Morocco.
Isabella and Angelina eat warm bread,
    drink hot chocolate, dress for school.

She inspects their nails before
    the nuns do. Abuela
cares for the girls after school.
    Cave dances, eager tourists,
she sees them in her mind's eye
    clapping and staring,

her hands raised in the Flamenco pose,
    clicking her fingers
in time to her long, loosely draped body,
    her electric response to the guitarra.
She hates their stares, feels like a parrot
    on show behind bars.

At the corner café she eats tapas,
    drinks wine after work.
Her voice rattles like parched gravel

in the corner courtyards
where the wind blows fiercely,
    from the Sierra Nevadas.

After a bottle, she hears her own
    contralto voice, a resonant sound,
remembers resting her head
    on her mother's warm stomach.
Most evenings, she smells alcohol,
    cigarettes, and sweat.

Her clothes reek of her,
    not washed for a week.
During her showers, local boys gawk
    over corrugated steel.
I am old wax, she remembers,
    melted down, nothing left to burn.

She imagines her parents strewing
    roses on her grave, lighting
candles to honor the dead. The girls
    wear necklaces with tiny gold
crosses. I am a turnip anchored to the earth,
    an enormous bat suspended, she broods.

She meets him at the market,
    buys pan, chorizo,

bolts of flannel smelling of the sun.
  He drinks espresso at a round table.
Older, grizzled, he catches her
  off guard with a word.

She carries the black coffee
  to his table.
I often come here for Mother's flannel.

The fabric of the old, he says,
  hard to keep warm
during the nights.

Are you a dancer?

Yes. We dance for the tourists
  in Grenada. He notes the swing to her long hair,
her toe tapping on the floor's sunny tile.

She later remembers his remark:
  ". . . hard to keep warm,"
feels the girls' arms heavy with sleep
reach around her in the dark.

Alfred Nicol

Drink & Dial

My ex, I recall, was pestered by such men.
Fixated, fraught, a man alone, possessed
Of a telephone, demanding she be the dream
To piece his broken sleep together.
                                    Who guessed
That I'd assume such habits, given time?
That if she let it ring I'd call again?

Here's what to do. Undaunted, leave a message.
Always be charming, even when you're not.
Charm's a thing that every loser's got.
Try to lose the stutter. Lose the edge.
Breathe in. Say something bright to the machine.
Picture yourself alert, composed, and lean.

You charge the phone that way with sheer potential.
It lasts for hours. A dozing animal,
The thing could leap to life! If not now. . . now!

Except she won't call. Etiquette won't allow.
Or, perhaps not etiquette exactly.
No, perhaps not etiquette at all.
A kind of horror. Horror, it might be.
She plays you back and finds you very small.

Alfred Nicol

The Gift

Quick as thought, the shortstop dives to snag
The blur of white, and though he's on his knees,
His strong peg beats the runner to the bag.
The gifted do what's difficult with ease.

Such music is clear water over stones.
So fluid are her hands upon the keys,
There springs a braided stream of sparkling tones.
The gifted do what's difficult with ease.

The couples link their arms along the pier,
Whispering under lanterns in the breeze.
Some few small words fall softly on the ear.
The gifted do what's difficult with ease.

Alfred Nicol

Guinea Pig

A pet, domesticated overmuch,
Inhabiting interminable lulls,
Most pusillanimous of animals,
Inertia's own, quiescent as the sands,
And shy to venture even round the hutch,
Her pleasure is a motor in my hands,
An instrument set racing with a touch.

A little thing of breath and heat compact,
Mildest of spirits, in a flask of fur,
Without even a sound as signature,
No bark or whinny, whistle or meow,
No word to instigate or to react,
She gently nods assent to here and now,
An answer well-considered and exact.

I'll learn from this one how much not to do;
How large a silence to accumulate;
To serve with those who only stand and wait,
To change alfalfa, sawdust, water, salt,
For other needs as moderate and few;
To thrill when lifted; visited, exalt;
Nor ever speak till I be spoken through.

_____

His and Hers

He kept the truck, drove out to western Mass,
And she moved down the coast along Cape Ann.
She's gone like Alice through the looking glass
To find herself. Or find another man.
Or he's the one who left. Without her knowing
What end to make of it, he let time pass
Between them. Well, she kept her maiden name
For when it came to this: they both are going.
They'll mix and match, they're young, it's all the same.

I mean they're not like us, her collar turned
Up high beneath her chin, and both in sleeves
Despite the heat. Religious, or sun-burned,
You're like to think. God knows if she believes.
A burn's the better guess—though not the kind
One doesn't own because it comes unearned;
No accident. They're covered, both, from wrist
To throat to ankle, forward and behind,
With body art. There's not an inch they've missed.

It's hardly what you might call art, agreed.
But call it something else, call it tattoos.
It does take skill. It does express a need;

There's risk involved, commitment. Words we use
To speak of aspiration all apply.
And if you prick the flesh, does it not bleed?
There's no erasing. Has to be just so.
The pattern stays, no matter how or why
The choice was made, however long ago.

Inherent as stigmata, or birth-mark,
Into the flesh of her narrow back is etched
A stylized, stained glass window Joan of Arc,
The image of beatitude bewitched
And witness that the body is a temple.
Yet when they lay together in the dark,
His skin an iconography of flames
That would engulf them both, their need was simple.
The choirs of the body raised their names.

Slipping off the wedding bands won't do.
Though each avoids the other's dead end streets,
One cannot but associate the two,
Their images unclothed among the sheets,
Burning toward a kind of martyrdom.
Could be I'm speaking, now, of me and you.
The question may as well be yours and mine.
Who will embrace these bodies, when they come
So marked with an indelible design?

Alfred Nicol

Potatoes

"*What happens to a dream deferred?*"
—Langston Hughes

I.

French for potatoes is *les pommes de terre;*
Earth-apples: crisp, but lumps—not red, or spherical.
The soil is never burdened, like the air,
With song or mythic fruit that waxes lyrical.
And earth's not water. No reflection's there.
No orchard hangs inverted by some miracle.
Something subversive curls inside a term
That wants to bring the apple to the worm.

II.

Hard to believe my father ever young.
An ill-advised furrow ploughed under revery.
But when he dreamed, he must have dreamed among
The pines beyond the granite-walled periphery
A dream selected like a stone and flung
Back on these rock-strewn fields as what could never be.
One simple stone took root where it was clear:
It's possible to grow potatoes here.

III.

A penitent in burlap, the brown root
Shrivels with neglect, its blind eyes fingering
The darkness. Prayer without a myth is mute.
My father, off to work without malingering,
Did not look up to see forbidden fruit
Or question the forbidding one with hungering.
His fate excluded any willful plot.
Potatoes kept for seed were left to rot.

IV.

How old he came to be, the patient one,
Happy alone, behind the toolshed puttering
In the least likely soil, out of the sun,
Dry needles raked away. The pale wings fluttering
Among potato leaves—his dreamwork done—
Alight and flicker like a candle guttering.
These are my father's orchards, empty now.
The stones upon the hill resist the plough.

Sunday

In August, oaks are orchestras
In concert on the public greens.
The maestro bows to light applause.
The crickets tap their tambourines.

An easy, bright formality
Is visited upon the day.
Maidenly spirits serve us tea
And after clear the cups away.

To get us closer to the sky
We rest our dreams upon the grass.
The laundered clouds are piled so high
The branches will not let them pass.

A hawk's wide ploughshare tilts and tills
His cultivated fields of air.
The angels at their windowsills
Remark the weather passing fair.

Something's discovered in a day
Whose means are matched to gentle ends.
From a point of stillness far away,
A parable of light descends.

Alfred Nicol

Wide Brush

*"Vanity of vanities, says the Preacher;
all is vanity."*
— Ecclesiastes 12:8

Late afternoon, in the slant winter light,
Where men are painting the white buildings white,
The shadows of their ladders climb the walls
To meet the covering darkness as it falls.

Brian T. O'Brien

_____

Pantry Mouse

It is hard to say who was more surprised
at our encounter, you or I, though
I retained sufficient dignity
to avoid dropping pellets where I stood.

It was not the same for you, wee one,
wild-eyed, and terror-filled, shaking
to your very core, desperate enough
for a daytime raid on the pantry.

You, overmatched in size, if not in speed
and wit—I mortified that such a thing
would happen in my kitchen, which, while not
exactly spotless, was far from filthy—

stared at one another for an eternity
that wouldn't allow the "one chimpanzee"
metric to complete. A lifetime passed
in that second. Though I knew I wouldn't

harm you, neither did I want your presence.
In that frozen moment when both our minds
compacted to essentials, we agreed
to play out unwanted roles assigned us.

You slid with whatever dignity
you could muster down a vertical
partition, and I threatened and swore
like a man — though without conviction.

It was very much like when love departs.
There will be no traps or poisoned bait.
I put a brick in front of your hole,
as I did another time with my heart.

Brian T. O'Brien

Vespers: Canada Geese at the North Pool

Fifty-six by my certain count; that was
merely two off from my natal years;
I thought I'd spend some time in idle thought,
attempting to symbolize that number,

equate it with a chapter or a verse,
the days of a journey or a voyage,
a sacrificial peace offering, or a measure
of the ark—either nautical or covenantal.

I am no cabalist, though my sympathies
are with any quirky study that allows me
to believe some intelligence designed
this maddening world around me.

And then I knew that fifty-six was exactly right
for this congregate gaggle, clothed in sober colors
Benedict, Dominic, and Francis chose for their own:
white for purity, black for remembrance, brown for
    the earth.

They had, for the hour I had viewed them,
labored quietly and diligently under the eye

of some abbot, though I could not, with certainty,
ascertain which of several candidates he might be.

Each worked the winter wheat from soil or stalk,
either solitarily or in groups of six, seven —a dozen.
Then —moved by some unheard bell or claxon,
to a goose —their heads swung westward,

and in the glittering rays of the descending sun,
the community proclaimed itself at peace.
Had I heard Te Deum rendered in perfect Goose,
I would not have been more moved than I was

by their simple practiced elegance. It was
as natural as waddling, swimming, flying —yet
transcended such —as perfect tasks become prayers.
Perhaps, the real work of geese is worship.

Greg Perry

The Last Man Out of Parker
Wildlife Refuge 1984

They say the island hermit is just afraid
to be outgoing, still living there, some nerve,
upon a ragged sandbar, domain of deer
and waterfowl, a government preserve.
He'd rather live alone, like a renegade.
But Lew, if asked, would gladly volunteer
a different point of view, remembering when
the island was a neighborhood, a place
for names and faces, not a forsaken den
for migratory birds, or solitaire.
The lilac bushes are all that fill the space
familiar with that far-off yesterday.
It's not that Lew has left the human race.
It's just that everyone has moved away.

José Edmundo Ocampo Reyes

Ledger

In the antique dealer's book,
whose condition a bibliophile might rate as *good,*
hinges weak though binding remains tight, crack
starting to head of spine, a record of events
and corresponding changes to his bottom line,
not unlike a running tally
of how many soldiers an army's divisions lost
or killed: entries for the Jun Yao bowl
with purple splashes, but none
for the cobblestoned street outside,
an anonymous story written in the foot's Braille;
for the stolen scrimshaw tooth,
engraved with a three-masted ship,
and the shattered Venetian goblet,
but not for the mahogany bracket clock
with unmatched finials that a rival
dealer could not convince him to take;
for the crystal chandelier that graced
waltz after waltz after waltz,
but not for the clerk who came in
each noon and never bought a thing,
as if leafing through a dictionary
that lacked whatever word he had in mind;

for the Georgian naval dirk that shed
its first owner's blood, but not for the townspeople
robbed at knifepoint trying to cut through
the adjacent alley; for the Marklin train
and the die-cast Routemaster bus
no child will ever play with again,
but not for the fountain-pen aficionado
the dealer will never meet,
whose country is nowhere to be found
on the Victorian student's desk globe;
not for what he will never possess,
the azure-on-crimson *suzani* that took
a Shakhrisabz family months to embroider;
and not, certainly not, for the passersby
who peer into the window,
heedless of any possible connection
between the muted apparitions on the glass
and the dim interior of his store.

José Edmundo Ocampo Reyes

Paálam, Wallace, Paálam

One rejects / the trash.
"The Man on the Dump"

An an begins this poem, not a the,
yet it evokes a theme, one theme among
the myriad. Some perhaps are yours?
Part of me wants to indulge you and accept

your invitation to enter the quiet house,
become the large red man who ponders
a tome without blurbs...though I must decline.
Since the world I live in isn't calm,

I choose to be politic, not polite.
Your an is my the, the trash you've rejected—
core of the mango, grenade of sweetness;
rusty can, currency for food; words

merely syllables to your yawning ear.
(If French and English are a single language,
why aren't all tongues fungible?)
Even now my dump swells into a mountain,

garlands of wilting sampaguita strewn
along its slopes. Paálam, Wallace, paálam.
Somewhere on this planet is a sea
where thirteen gulls are drowning in black gold.

Deborah Warren

Aelfgyva

HIC DVX WILGELM CVM HAROLDO VENIT AD
PALATIVM SVVM VBI VNVS CLERICVS ET AELFGYVA
— The Bayeux Tapestry, 1070-1080

Out of nowhere onto the strip of linen
Aelfgyva descends into the story.
Not her story: William of Normandy's
and Edward the Confessor's — it belongs
more to Harold of Wessex's hawk and hounds
than to the girl who springs into the scene
at the blue and yellow castle in Rouen
where a certain cleric and Aelfgyva — what?

We've all had an Aelfgyva-at-the-palace.
In she jumps unushered some dull Monday
abrupt as luck — no thread of exposition
offered in advance — and disappears
before her sentence even gets its verb;
and yet we're stuck with her. She's something worse
than unexplained or sudden, a thing unfinished
that needles you and gets under your skin

and pricks you to embroider her an ending,
marry or kill her off — or anything
but keep her, flanked by dragon-headed pillars,

scarlet-wimpled, maddening and hanging
there, beside her cleric, as a question
you can neither sew up or unsew.
But keep her. She's the thing you need the most —
more than the things you can completely know.

Deborah Warren

The Crabapple in Flower

The crabapple tore through the house one week in April,
boughs in armloads—room after room—in vases,
jars from the cupboards, jugs from the cellar, urns.
By what ploy did an artless flower come
—white and pink, red bud and country leaf—
laying siege to the heart of our existence?

Something to do with disparity—the flower
brief and new on the gnarled neglected branch.
And something else. The long sprays dazzled us,
but their beauty pierced us, too, with a desire
to know them, to possess them, in some way
five pale senses could never satisfy.

Deborah Warren

Elizabeth's Dress

Elizabeth's dress was not the red of claret,
not maroon or amethyst or rose.
Vermilion? Not exactly. Was it scarlet?
Ruby? Poppy? Crimson? None of those.

I can have you read the way the velvet
poured itself around her narrow ankles —
tell you how it showed her shoulders: What
I *can't* describe (except by saying *not*
and cataloguing everything it wasn't)
would make it flesh and blood and living — but
a thing like color? Dim description doesn't
splash you with the dye that dyed the dress
or turn your head or make you catch your breath —
and if I could make you see its shade of red,
I still could not describe Elizabeth.

Deborah Warren

Gibbon Motion

difficilior lectio

Look at the the motion of the lucky gibbon,
pouring himself like liquid on the limb
he streams along—less animal than oil—
gliding as if there's nothing more to him
than motion. Stone-hard underneath the gibbon's
bright glissade, do aches and agonies
like mine cramp at his heart while he's sashaying
easy and elastic in the trees?

If that's the way we ought to read the gibbon,
giving him fears and headaches he suppresses,
you're like him—like me: For all your flowing
clear as water, I should look at you
guessing what's underneath your easy going
and reading you as complicated, too.

Deborah Warren

Roof-Walker

He leans on the sky up there, as if he's painting
not so much the rust-streaked silver roof
as the shed, the field, the sun—the whole July—
with strokes of barn-red, hay-green, sky-blue air.
Maybe the scene's so blazing-summer dry
you wonder about the reason for the rust;
but think of the Januaries that he's there
sweeping a white mass over the eaves below.
And wonder, then, if you could get accustomed
(up there between the silver or the snow
and heaven) to the roof and to the sky,
to brushing the weather away—and if you'd grow
too seasoned in the barn-roof point of view
to come back down to the flat brown earth you knew.

Deborah Warren

Thrift Shop

Seven flannel nightgowns, nearly new;
and I'm the flannel type. Besides, the price
was dirt-cheap, at three dollars each; and they
were made for someone just my height. But who
would wear and wash new nightgowns once or twice
and give them —hardly ever worn —away?

You know, as well as I do, who —well, why
suddenly seven nightgowns with their nap
still blooming on the flannel would be sold.
Not because some young girl thought she'd try
something alluring —like spaghetti straps
or satin. No; the flannel type is old.

And she, I think, is more than old. And wizened
down to mere thin bones, she wears the height
we have in common like a negligée
of flesh so sheer —transparent —that it isn't
there at all. Dirt-cheap; and now each night
reminds me to be thrifty with my days.

Deborah Warren

What the Dolphins Know

> *iam nostros curvi norunt delphines amores*
> —Leander Heroni (Heroïdes, Ovid)

Think how heavy the water was, and Sestos
far—too far to swim to every evening;
but Leander swam along a highway
blazed by habit, as if his arms, like wheels,
had beaten a liquid road in a salty thicket.
Fish, his intimates and his familiars,
sang to him, and the dolphins that dove beside him
knew the boy—all head and heel and elbow—
who grasped the sea in handfuls and pulled not water
toward his heart with his curving hands, but love.

Whether Hero forgot to light the pine-torch,
whether a hurricane tore out the fire,
whether leaping whitecaps concealed the lighthouse
doesn't matter. What I know is this:
Love is an element where thrashing strangers
bend their limbs to a medium not their own.

Maybe, if you're a lover, you're Leander
paving a path in a rolling patch of ocean.
Or you're a dolphin, beached on a stony pasture,
fins entangled in grass and ragweed—flailing—

rising—arching over the dust and pollen.
If you climb on the sky, your fingers clutching
emptiness, if your legs take hold on nothing,
then I recognize you—the way the dolphins
knew Leander, knowing it takes a lover
to race with the creatures curving through the sea.

Richard Wollman

A Cemetery Affair

*[T]he oldest cemetery in use in Europe...was deeded to the
Juifs du Pape, the Jews who lived in Carpentras under the
protection of the Avignon popes....[In] 1990, a group of
people scaled the cemetery wall, toppled thirty-four grave
stones, and then proceeded to dig up the grave of an old
Jewish rug merchant named Felix Germon, who had died,
peacefully, that April.*

<u>The New Yorker</u>, November 6, 2000

I know your name, Felix Germon,
and know that you may not speak to me.
So begins what may turn out to be sin
if I disturb the garden cemetery
deeded to the Jews of Carpentras,
where you were unearthed before a star
was sewn into your skin.

I've seen the yellow star in the clothing
of those who wore it while they lived
and went about their way before it sank
into the flesh. I see a tilted slab turned by time,
a sign hanging from your neck —
it says, From the neighbors,
taken from another grave, out of context.

In Newburyport, while we sleep
someone barricades our door

with the neighbors' discarded Christmas trees,
their heavy trunks still oozing with sap.
A flash makes a skeleton of the bedroom,
and I think it's lightning, but know
later that we had been seen, a picture taken
before the voices left.

And the evening took silent hold of me
to hear the stitching, the work of quiet fingering.
Did he lean his hand against you
to ease the strain of the meticulous task?
I hear the creak of upturned stone,
smell the earth's breath as you are exhumed,
and wonder why this night, no different
from other nights, makes me afraid
to leave my son sleeping in a room
where stars we've strewn across the ceiling
begin to lose light.

It wasn't hard for the Catholics of Carpentras
to climb over the garden wall
when they courted *chez les Juifs*,
a cemetery affair they used to call it,
as they lay down together in the uncut grass
next to the wild oaks surrounding the burial plots
of the *Juifs du Pape*, the dead who waited
in caskets with holes drilled in the bottom
to let their bodies return to earth.

As it rains, a few old Jews lock the gate
while the summer darkens Carpentras.
My son has night fears, sees twins in his sleep
identical as they cleave, and he dreams
he's home only to wake in a strange room.
In the small yard of this house we've taken
a patch of grass is coming in despite a drought
that's lasted weeks. It rains across the peaks
where lightning strikes Mont Ventoux.

And I tend someone else's garden,
watch the water splash from side to side
and catch the light at the edge of the stones
giving proof of an essence that can't be grasped.
My son sees the flash and calls me in.

The luxuriance of your untended garden
throws shadows on the broken stones
near your mound of upturned earth.
Vines tighten their grip around the trees
until they have no choice but to cooperate
with their own end. I see a Catholic girl
on the Paris streets, your wife who said,
*He pleased me—what could I do but keep him
from the boxcars when they left Drancy?*

I've seen the multitudes of stars
and one made of skin,

a cold shroud of earth around me.
Are you cold where you are?
What is the seal upon thine arm?
A bracelet of hair gently twined there.
Could one be sufficient to repair the song?
May one star sing if the rest can't be heard?
Where were you when the universe was made?

I was with my son to ease his sleep,
not afraid of death for those who enter
uninitiated and lose themselves
in an ecstasy that figures the union
                of the cherubim.
I can't speculate on an unknown name,
though yours, Felix, is the fortunate pain
that lifts a cloak from one who's freed
and this night has again begun to sing.

Richard Wollman

The Evidence of Things Unseen

Fontaine-de-Vaucluse

Up and down the walk, bending with the river,
the crowd clattered and slapped,
looking for images to match what was in their books.
I was beneath them on the bank of the Sorgue,
staring at water so translucent—
no depths out of eye's reach.

    A mile up the path
Jacques Cousteau sent an electric eye
a thousand feet down
to plumb the source of the resurgent spring.
The probe exploded before it reached the sandy bed
without disturbing the quiet pool

      where Petrarch had a vision,
real as his own breath,
and in his seclusion must have known
why the eye is a sad traveler.

Contributors

David Berman is an attorney from Belmont, Massachusetts, who studied with Archibald MacLeish and Robert Lowell while attending Harvard Law School. He has published three poetry chapbooks: *Future Imperfect* (State Street Press, 1982), *Slippage* (Robert L. Barth, 1996), and *Greatest Hits 1965-2002* (Pudding House Publications, 2003).

Patricia Callan, a graduate of Boston University and Lesley University, is a poet and playwright living in Massachusetts and Florida. Her play, "Papa's House," won the Loren Taylor Playwriting Contest and was produced in Illinois. Her poems have been published in *Voices Volumes I and II, Sea Sands* and *Candelabrum* (UK). Before becoming a writer, she was a choral director and voice teacher.

Michael Cantor's work has appeared in *Iambs & Trochees, The Formalist, The Dark Horse* (UK), *The Atlanta Review, Candelabrum* (UK), *The Comstock Review* (Pushcart nomimation), *The Cumberland Review* (Robert Penn Warren Award finalist), *Edge City Review, Light Quarterly, Orbis* (UK) and many other journals and anthologies. His poem in this collection, "The Young Men in Their Beauty," was the 2004 winner of the Newburyport Art Association Poetry Award.

Bill Coyle lives in Somerville, Massachusetts, and teaches in the Writing Center at Salem State College. His poems and translations have appeared in *The Dark Horse* (UK), *The Formalist, The Hudson Review, The New Criterion, The New Republic* and *Poetry*. Mr. Coyle's work is included in *Phoenix Rising: The Next Generation Of American Formal Poets*.

Robert W. Crawford was born in 1958 in Philadelphia, Pennsylvania. He graduated from Colby College in 1980 and earned an MA at The George Washington University in 1985. From 1983 to 1994 he worked in and around the Pentagon, where, among other things, he provided support for worldwide exercises. He now lives and works in Chester, New Hampshire where he teaches poetry and directs the information technology department at Chester College of New England. His poems have been published in *The Formalist, The Dark Horse* (UK), *First Things, Forbes, The Comstock Review* and other national journals. *Too Much Explanation Can Ruin a Man*, his first book of poetry, was published in March, 2005 by David Robert Books.

Rhina P. Espaillat has published three chapbooks, *Mundo y Palabra/The World & The Word* (Oyster River Press, 2001), *RPE: Greatest Hits 1942-2001* (Pudding House Publications, 2003), and *The Story-teller's Hour* (Scienter Press, 2004), as well as five full-length poetry collections: *Lapsing to Grace* (Bennett & Kitchel, 1992), *Where Horizons Go* (New Odyssey Press, 1998), *Rehearsing Absence* (The University of Evansville Press, 2001), *The Shadow I Dress In* (David Robert Books, 2004) and *Playing at Stillness* (Truman State University Press, 2005). Dominican by birth, Espaillat has also published essays in both English and her native Spanish, as well as translations and short stories. Among her honors are the T. S. Eliot Prize in Poetry, The Richard Wilbur Award, three of the Poetry Society of America's annual prizes, two Howard Nemerov Awards, and the "Tree at My Window" Award from the Robert Frost Foundation.

Lois Frankenberger is a publicist and mother of two grown children. She was born and raised in Pennsylvania, graduated from Smith College with a BA in English, and lived in New York and Connecticut before moving to Andover, Massachusetts.

Midge Goldberg grew up in Florida and attended Yale University. She currently lives in Derry, New Hampshire, with her children, Hannah and Ely. She is an educational software designer and is studying for an MFA at the University of New Hampshire. Her poetry has been accepted for publication in such journals as *Yankee, Dogwood, Pivot,* and the Longman anthology *European Romantic Poetry.*

A.M. Juster is the author of a book of Petrarch translations, *Longing for Laura* (Birch Brook Press 2002), and *The Secret Language of Women* (University of Evansville Press, 2003). He has been a featured poet in *Light* and is a two-time winner of the Howard Nemerov Sonnet Award. His work has appeared in *The Paris Review, Carolina Quarterly* and the *Michigan Quarterly Review.* He teaches on an adjunct basis at Emerson College.

Merrill Kaitz is the author of *The Great Boston Trivia and Fact Book.* A former Peace Corps volunteer (Seoul), his poems, stories and reviews have appeared in *Ploughshares, Dark Horse, Zeugma, The Boston Phoenix, The Boston Globe,* and elsewhere. An expert Scrabble player who lives in Amesbury, MA, he is also, at times, a caped crusader for peace, justice, and eros.

Don Kimball is a retired family therapist living in Concord, NH. His poetry has appeared in *The Formalist, The Lyric, Edge City Review, Iambs & Trochees, Blue Unicorn* and various other journals. His poems also appear in several recent anthologies, including *Fashioned Pleasures,* a chapbook of Bout Rimes based on a Shakespearean sonnet.

Elaine Kimball has been involved in community theater for 30 years, acting, directing and producing plays, and writing several musical reviews. Her life-long interest in local history and archaeology has led her to serve as dig director on several important digs, help to secure passage of the bill that established the office of Massachusetts State Archaeologist, and serve on the Board of Directors for the Archaeological Society. She recently retired after working 20 years in child protective services. Her work has appeared in *The Atlantic Monthly* and other journals.

Len Krisak has taught at Brandeis, Northeastern University, and Stonehill College. His two chapbooks, *Midland* and *Fugitive Child*, came out in 1999 from Somers Rocks Press and Aralia Press, respectively. In 2000, his full-length collection *Even as We Speak* won the Richard Wilbur Prize and was published by the University of Evansville Press. In 2004, *If Anything* appeared from WordTech Editions, and in 2006, Carcanet will publish his *Complete Odes of Horace*. His work has appeared over the years in *Agenda, Commonweal, The Hudson Review, PN Review, The Formalist, The National Review, Margie, Tennessee Quarterly, Classical Outlook, Pivot, Rattapallax, The Weekly Standard,* and *The Oxford Book of Poems on Classical Mythology,* among many others. In addition to the Richard Wilbur Prize, he has received the Robert Penn Warren and Robert Frost Prizes, along with numerous awards from the New England Poetry Club, the Los Angeles Poetry Festival, and over 50 other organizations. He is the former winner of the GoldPocket.com National Trivia Competition and is a four-time Champion on *Jeopardy!*

Michele Leavitt is a former trial attorney who now teaches in The Writing Program at the University of North Florida in Jacksonville. Her poems and essays have been published in a variety of journals and anthologies, including *Rattapallax, The Humanist, Wind, Yellow Silk II: International Erotic Stories and Poems,* and *The Edge City Review.*

Nancy Bailey Miller is a violinist originally from New York. She has published three books: *Dance Me Along the Path* (Strathmoor Books, 1996), *Of Minitmen & Molly's* (Strathmoor Books, 2002), and *Before the Dove Returns* (Strathmoor Books, 2004). Anthologized in *Our Mothers and Our Selves,* Miller's poetry has also appeared in *Rattapallax, Mediphors, Blue Unicorn* and *Arts North,* among other journals. Miller currently works at Phillips Academy Andover, where she teaches writing and manages the Chapel office.

James Najarian grew up on a goat farm in Pennsylvania. He has a PhD from Yale and teaches nineteenth-century British literature at Boston College. He has published a critical study, *Victorian Keats* (Palgrave MacMillan, 2002), as well as verse in *Ararat, Blue Unicorn, Folio,* and *The Mennonite.*

Mildred J. Nash studied with Elizabeth Bishop, Robert Lowell and Robert Fitzgerald at Harvard, before beginning a teaching career in the Burlington (MA) school system, from which she has recently retired. She is the author of *Beyond Their Dreams* (Pocahontas Press, 1989).

Karen Nelson lives in Newton, NH, where she writes poetry, teaches elementary school children, and paints. She also teaches creative writing through the Newburyport Adult Education program. Her poems have appeared in *The Larcom Review, Peregrine, Earth's Daughters, California Quarterly,* and the publication of The Poetry Society of New Hampshire, *The Poet's Touchstone.*

Alfred Nicol was recipient of the 2004 Richard Wilbur Award for his first book of poems, *Winter Light*, published by The University of Evansville Press. His poems have been anthologized in *Contemporary Poetry of New England* and in *Sonnets: 150 Contemporary Sonnets*, and have appeared in *Commonweal, The New England Review, The Formalist, Measure* and other journals. A serialization of his long poem, "Persnickety Ichabod's Rhyming Diary" appears in *Light Quarterly*.

Brian O'Brien, a very early member of the Powow River Poets, has published work in *Garden Lane* and has a poetry collection out looking for a publisher. He has taught at Tufts, Northeastern University, Merrimack College and UMass/Lowell. He is an editor of technical documentation, has run his own firm and managed a group of technical editors, and currently does management technology consulting for Shiman Associates in Boston.

Greg Perry has been a member of the Powow River Poets since 1994, and credits the organization with saving his life at that time. These days, he can be found on his website "grapez," a poetry blog and natural ramble. He is also blogging for Mr. Henry Thoreau, posting daily entries from the journals on "The Blog of Henry David Thoreau."

José Edmundo Ocampo Reyes was born and raised in the Philippines, and holds degrees from Ateneo de Manila and Columbia Universities. His poems and translations have appeared in such journals as *Circumference, The Hudson Review, Michigan Quarterly Review, Natural Bridge, Philippine Studies, Ploughshares,* and *Rattle,* and have been featured on *Poetry Daily*. He is the recipient of the Der-Hovanessian Translation Prize from the New England Poetry Club, the Richard Lemon

Scholarship from the Napa Valley Writers Conference, and the Walker Scholarship from the Fine Arts Work Center in Provincetown, MA.

Deborah Warren was born in Boston and educated at Harvard. After 15 years teaching Latin and English, and 10 years as a software engineer, she and her husband, who have 9 children, now raise heifers on a farm in Vermont while living in Andover, Massachusetts. Her work has appeared in numerous magazines, including *The Hudson Review*, *The New Criterion*, *Paris Review* and *Yale Review*. Her two collections of poetry are *The Size of Happiness* (Waywiser Press, 2003) and *Zero Meridian* (Ivan R. Dee, 2004), which won the 2004 New Criterion Prize. Ms. Warren has been the recipient of the Robert Penn Warren Prize, the Howard Nemerov Sonnet Award, and the Robert Frost Award.

Richard Wollman is the author of *Evidence of Things Seen* (Sheep Meadow Press, 2005) and *A Cemetery Affair* (Finishing Line Press, 2004). Winner of the 2005 Gulf Coast Prize in Poetry, he has published poems in *New England Review*, *Prairie Schooner*, *Crazyhorse*, and *Poetry Daily*. He teaches Renaissance literature and Creative Writing at Simmons College in Boston and lives in Newburyport, MA with his wife and son.

Acknowledgments

DAVID BERMAN. "After a Family Reunion" originally appeared in *Counter Measures* and was reprinted in *Greatest Hits* (Pudding House Publications, 2003). "Disjunctures" and "Future Imperfect" are from *Greatest Hits*. "Progressions of the Mind" first appeared in *Sparrow*. Reprinted with the permission of the author.

MICHAEL CANTOR. "Japanese for Beginners" appeared in *Atlanta Review*. "Poem Noir" and "The Disappearance" appeared in *The Cumberland Review* and "The Young Men in Their Beauty" in *Iambs & Trochees*. Reprinted with the permission of the author.

BILL COYLE. "Anima" first appeared in *The Formalist*. "Leave Taking" first appeared in *Dark Horse*, "The Moons of Earth" first appeared in *The New Republic*, and "Tjelvars Grav" first appeared in *Poetry*. "The God of This World to His Prophet" and "The Magic Circle" first appeared in *The Hudson Review*. Reprinted with the permission of the author.

ROBERT CRAWFORD. "French Braids" first appeared in *The Cumberland Poetry Review*. "Power Failure" and "The Whole of It" first appeared in *The Formalist*. "A Row of Stones" first appeared in *The Comstock Review*. "Salisbury Cathedral" first appeared in *The Lyric*. "Town Roads" first appeared in *The Dark Horse*. All of the poems were reprinted in *Too Much Explanation Can Ruin A Man* (David Roberts Books, 2005), where "The Swearing In of Calvin Coolidge" first appeared. Reprinted with the permission of the author.

RHINA P. ESPAILLAT. "Butchering" first appeared in *Margie*. "Encounter," which first appeared in *The Lyric*, "Hang Gliders," which first appeared in *Orbis*, and "Highway Apple Trees," which first appeared in *Galley Sail Review*, were all reprinted in *Lapsing To Grace* (Bennett & Kitchel, 1992). "If You Ask Me," which first appeared in *Medicinal Purposes,* and "Weighing In," which first appeared in *America,* were reprinted in *Where Horizons Go* (New Odyssey Press, 1998). "My Cluttered House Accuses Me of Greed" first appeared in *Medicinal Purposes* and was reprinted in *The Shadow I Dress In* (David Robert Books, 2004). "There Is a Man" first appeared in *Pivot* and was reprinted in *Rehearsing Absence* (The University of Evansville Press, 2001). "Vignette" first appeared in *Poetry.* Reprinted with the permission of the author.

MIDGE GOLDBERG. "The Fish" and "The Flume Ride" first appeared in *Dogwood.* "Town Parade" fist appeared in *Pivot.* Reprinted with the permission of the author.

A. M. JUSTER. "Cancer Prayer" first appeared in *Edge City Review.* "Letter to Auden" first appeared in *Light.* "Moscow Zoo" and "Note to Echo" first appeared in *The Formalist.* "Visions of the Serengeti" first appeared in *Paris Review.* All of these poems were reprinted in *The Secret Language of Women* (The University of Evansville Press, 2003), where "Los Periquitos" first appeared. Reprinted with the permission of the author.

DON KIMBALL. "Deer in a Craft Shop" first appeared in the *Schuylkill Valley Journal of the Arts.* "Milk Can" first appeared in *The Formalist.* Reprinted with the permission of the author.

LEN KRISAK. "Birds from Afar " and "A Version of Akhmatova" first first appeared in *Even as We Speak* (The University of Evansville Press, 2000). "Constance Marvin" and "Mrs. Henley" first appeared in *Midland* (Somers Rocks Press, 1999) and were reprinted in *Even as We Speak.* "Day-Schoolers on a Walk" appeared in *The Formalist* and was reprinted in *Even as We Speak.* "On Finishing a Translation of Ovid's Amores" first appeared in *The Formalist* and was reprinted in *If Anything* (WordTech Editions, 2004), where "Common," "Plumbing Emergency," and "What of the Night?" first appeared. Reprinted with the permission of the author.

MICHELE LEAVITT. "Charm School" first appeared in *The Merrimack Literary Review*. "Ladies Night" first appeared in *Main Street Rag*. Reprinted with the permission of the author.

NANCY BAILEY MILLER. "Noah's Wife" first appeared in *Before The Dove Returns* (Strathmoor Books, 2004). Reprinted with the permission of the author.

MILDRED NASH. "Hera, Elderly" first appeared in *Visions*. "North Country Graveyard" and "Vineyard Conjuring" first appeared in *Yankee*. Reprinted with the permission of the author.

ALFRED NICOL. "Drink & Dial," "His and Hers," and "Potatoes" first appeared in *Winter Light* (The University of Evansville Press, 2004). "Guinea Pig" first appeared in *Commonweal* and was reprinted in *Winter Light*. "Sunday" and "Wide Brush" first appeared in *Rattapallax* and were reprinted in *Winter Light*. "The Gift" first appeared in *Schuylkill Valley Journal of the Arts*. Reprinted with the permission of the author.

BRIAN O'BRIEN. "Vespers" first appeared in *Garden Lane*. Reprinted with the permission of the author.

GREGORY PERRY. "The Last Man Out of Parker Wildlife Refuge 1984" first appeared in *Bellowing Ark*. Reprinted with the permission of the author.

JOSÉ EDMUNDO OCAMPO REYES. "Ledger" first appeared in *The Hudson Review*. Reprinted with the permission of the author.

DEBORAH WARREN. "Aelfgyva," which first appeared in *Runes*, "Elizabeth's Dress," which first appeared in *Iambs & Trochees*, and "Thrift Shop," which first appeared in *Mandrake*, were reprinted in *The Size of Happiness* (The Waywiser Press, 2003). "The Crabapple in Flower," which first appeared in *The Hudson Review*, "Gibbon Motion," which first appeared in *Yale*

Review, and "What the Dolphins Know," which first appeared in *The Leviathan Quarterly,* were reprinted in *Zero Meridian* (Ivan R. Dee, 2004), where "Roof-Walker" first appeared. Reprinted with the permission of the author.

RICHARD WOLLMAN. "A Cemetery Affair," and "Evidence of Things Seen" are both from *Evidence of Things Seen* (forthcoming in 2005 from Sheep Meadow Press) and are also in *A Cemetery Affair* (Finishing Line Press, 2004). Reprinted with the permission of the author.